AF362506

Harmony in Lost Puzzle Pieces

Her Many Thoughts

BookLeaf Publishing

India | USA | UK

Harmony in Lost Puzzle Pieces © 2022 Her
Many Thoughts

All rights reserved.

No part of this publication may be
reproduced, stored in a retrieval system, or
transmitted, in any form or by any means,
electronic, mechanical, photocopying,
recording or otherwise, without the prior
written permission of the presenters.

Her Many Thoughts asserts the moral right
to be identified as author of this work.

Presentation by *BookLeaf Publishing*

Web: www.bookleafpub.com

E-mail: info@bookleafpub.com

ISBN: 9789357443999

First edition 2022

DEDICATION

To my younger self, well done!

Look at how far you've come.

ACKNOWLEDGEMENT

All praise and thanks to God the Al-Mighty, who I couldn't have done this without.

I'd also like to thank my family and friends who encouraged me to complete this project (and to this day continue to support me).

And finally, I'd like to show my gratitude to the little girl who deep-down inside didn't give up believing in herself. You did it, girl!

PREFACE

Dear Readers,

Thanks for picking this up.

I hope you enjoy reading these 21-poems.

Please note that they were written as part of a 21-day challenge. Yes, I had 21 days to craft the contents of this book!

Despite this, one thing remains true: I needed a nudge, and this was it! And I wasn't going to let this go!

Happy reading!

Much love,
Her Many Thoughts

Time

Ever since I was young,
I thought I had way too much time.

Now that I'm older - and somewhat wiser
I realise I can't have been more wrong.

There's so much to do, so little time
I've grown to accept that it's necessary to juggle
time.

I tell myself, I'll be fine.
That I really know how to prioritise and organise
my life,
but do I really? Or is that a lie I tell myself?

You see everyone says prioritise
But how do I know what deserves the spotlight?

How do I know what's important?
And what's not?
What's worth it?
And what's not?

How do I figure that all out?

I guess I should pause briefly.

Take a breath.

One.
    Breathe.
        Two...Breathe..
            Three...
    ...Four...

.......Five...

Easy.

But wait!

What comes next? What do I do now?
Oh, it's getting late.

I must hurry.

Life is fleeting.

It doesn't seem to be slowing.

When I was younger,
I thought time passed so slowly.
I wished it away.

I think my wish came true.

Well, it took its time,
'cos while I was younger I couldn't wait.

And now that I'm older I think I'm too slow.

I'm not catching up. I'm behind.
At the end of the line.

And now, all I can do is to wish for it to slow
down.

I want to take it all in.
I want to savour it.
I want. To take. My. Time.

And I will.

Sure, it passes by so quickly...
...but I will.

Everything begins with a step.

And here's mine.

One.

2021

Twenty twenty-one
What a year this has been, right?
It's second to none?

Well, that's true for some
The world we all love and know
in groups divided

To some, they lost all
others, some of what they knew
and the lucky won
 - jackpot!

Yet, to many...

It was another
2020 version two
Oh, see what a year

What a year
Was twenty-twenty one

And what a year
Will twenty-twenty two
become?

Run get that money, run spend it all

I want to see dollar signs
But I am blind

I want to build an empire
But I am tired

I want to go the distance
But I am lost

That's £9.99

Coffee and cake
Milk and bread
Toilet paper
Clothes

Cash or card?

Today I learnt
 capitalism is a never-ending cycle

Maybe I knew this from before

It brings me comfort, but that comfort of feeling makes me
feel discomfort. So, to feel comfortable, I'll turn to my vices and
I'll search for some form of calm and warmth.

Only to find it in things that will eventually destroy me

TLC

Pop the kettle on
Grab your mug
Now brew your tea

Light a candle
Dim the lights
Put your hair up

Draw a bath
Lay out your clothes
Moisturise your skin

Plump up that pillow
Straighten the sheets
Spritz your sweet scent

Put your feet up
Open your book
Dive right in

Ayeeyo, I miss you

I just didn't think
It'd be so soon.

I'd love to
hear your warm laugh
see your gentle face
smell your sweet scent
Feel your soft skin

I want to go on another trip with you
To fly over unknown countries with you
I'd kill to eat from the world with you
Oh, what I'd give to sip tea with you

I want to make you toast
I want to make you a bowl of porridge – no
honey!
I want to listen to your stories
I want to check your blood sugars

…

But I know you're somewhere better
I know you've made it to the other side

God willing, you are happy right now

I can't be selfish

So, I let you go

But I know I'll meet you soon.

Who am I?

Old
Kind
Reckless
Impatient
Pretty
Young
Fat
Friend
Bold
Funny
Daughter
Believer
Teacher
Sister
Selfless
Spender
Sinner
Rebel
Quirky
Messy
Cold
Awkward

Who am I?

Am I just a girl,
born to girl,
who was married to a son of a girl?

Who am I?
Am I a person
Who pretends to endure the struggle
To work hard and party harder?

Who am I?
Am I an imposter,
Born to migrants in search of a better life?

Who am I?
It doesn't really matter
Who I am. Because, who I'll become
Is a much more poignant question.

As who I am is constantly changing

Mercy

Mercy

Mankind
Eats and
Repeats this
Cycle
Yearly

AND

Making
Everything
Revolve
Crazily around
Yourself

IS

Manifesting some
Energy and
Releasing it
Chaotically into the

YOU-niverse

Believe me, I know we should be selfish…but
not everything is always about you.

Think of others.

Have some mercy, please.

Hearts

From my lips to yours
My soul reaches out
For a connection

Entwined in tablets
Long-ago prescribed
Our paths were
Meant to cross and unite

Just for a time
To enjoy frivolously
Like children
Innocently

Womanhood

Womanhood
Defined as the state of being a woman
From where a young girl
Grows and transforms into a lady

But what makes me a woman…

Is it my physical being
My body
My shape
My voice

Or it my essence
The way I carry myself
What I choose to do
Who and how I interact

I understand privilege is varied
From city to city, Country and borders

How I'm treated, where I walk
Is often linked to the way I talk
And might I add, to the way I dress

Some see me as oppressed, but let me stress
It's a choice, I assure you it is. I am as free to
remove it
As I am to don it. But I appreciate not everyone
is as fortunate as me
But this does not mean you can talk for me, or
others in a similar situation as I.

Let us be.

If you don't like, you don't like.

I can't force you to smile or even ask you to fake
one.

What I do know is you shouldn't be put in
charge,
Or should I say determine what my womanhood
should or should not reveal

That choice is entirely mine

It's as simple as ABC and 123

100 Days

Take a deep breath, it'll be fine.
You will be OK.

Don't stress...don't worry.
Just try your best.

It's fine. It's alright.
Everything works out in the end, right?

Kunai and Shuriken

Determination
it is one of your strongest traits,
and I admire it.

So is your empathy,
It's like you have a sixth sense, a tingle
A sort of spidey-sense for all the feels.

I find it commendable that you do,
but let that not get to your head.

Despite all your mistakes and shortcomings,
I must admit
you do eventually realise you were wrong.
Sometimes this takes
Forever
but even then
you still apologise

When you were born,
a day marked with love,
My life would never be the same

Thank you, for knowing when
to put your kunai and shuriken
Away.

The curious case of Mr Malink

I just want you to know
You are beautiful
Inside and out
You truly are

Indeed
You are Mr Handsome
Mr Dapper

You are smart and funny

But I wonder, what's happened to all your
wonder?
Where did that zeal go? Did that passion fly
away?
That thirst for knowledge – is it hiding?

Your hunger for knowledge
seems to be satisfied by quick fixes nowadays,
for easy rewards and predictable
outcomes are not it

No longer do you pose questions
for things you yearn to understand

You seem to just accept it all
As it is

There's no fun in that!

Deep down
I see a flicker of light
It's small
It's humble
It's shy

But it's there.

Ignite it.

Set it aflame.

Come back and rise like the phoenix you are.

The Cringe Factor

Why?
Why would I say that?
What possessed me?

I'm such a weirdo.

I mean, how do I always end up in the same
sh-…
It's like it's my own-personal comedic shtick

Wait a minute, it's not that bad.
Calm down. It's in all your head.

But seriously, WHY?

People 'forgetting' is all a lie,
Whoever said people don't notice
Was blind
to the fact that people enjoy seeing others
distressed

I am in charge of how I think of myself
So, I guess I should be able to change that!
At least?

But then here I lie awake
Wondering why I'm being plagued
With re-runs of the same event
that happened so long ago
All at 3am?

These experiences are replaying rent-free in my
head
They're occupying valuable land
(I could be doing so much more right about
now)

It's as though these ghosts
Enjoy taunting me

Seriously though, why?!

I have a list

I have a list,
It's a really long list:

A list of things I'd like to achieve

A list of places I'd like to visit

A list of foods I'd to eat

A list of films I'd like to watch

A list of chores I need to complete

A list of books I need to read

A list of items I need to buy

A list of meals I'd like to try and make

But my lists have now turned into

Lists of places that no longer exist

Lists of people I cannot meet

Lists of things I've not achieved by when I said

And lists of things I've lost

I drink tea, coffee and boba
<3

I drink tea
To warm my body
and heal my soul

I'll have a cup of chamomile
An hour or so before I KO

I might have a minty-tea
As a treat after a heavy meal

When I'm feeling adventurous
I'll have a nice hot cocoa
With a dash of cream
(and a marshmallow, added guilt-free!)

In the mornings, it's become my ritual
To whisk a teaspoon and half
of matcha, and add it to half a cup of milk
(oat or coconut - whatever's in the fridge)

A more recent discovery
Has been my love for boba
It's more of a sweet treat
On a hot summer's day

But one thing, I can't forgo
Is my daily dose of caffeine
In the form of coffee

I'll take two or three cups, please
I'll even drive to a local coffee shop

It's my drug, and I'm an addict.

The real struggle

I can't hear you!
                Thumbs twiddle.

Er, sorry, can you say that again?
                Look at your nails.

You're on mute?
                That spot on the wall looks
different.

Can you see my screen?
                Let me minimise this window.

Ok, let's move on to…
                I really need to pee.

Bees and other buzzing things

Buzz buzz goes the bee
The bee that was near the tree
The tree that swayed in front of me
Me, who stood there silently.

Buzz buzz goes the bee
The bee that produces honey for free
Honey made without a fee
Which we claim so carelessly.

Buzz buzz goes the bee
I see it slow down,
this little bumblebee

As it gets closer to my window I feel,
Another buzz buzz, coming from me.
It's my phone, another delivery.

I look away, guilty.

My Strong Sturdy Tree and Little December Moon (Sisters)

When I look at my reflection,
I see you both.

I feel that we're a mirror of each other.

Individuals, yes,
But not exactly.
Perhaps, iterations?
Reconstructed versions?

I'm not sure,
but I'd like to thank Hoyoo.
For without her,
there'd be no you.
Without her,
there'd be no me,

You both don't realise,
The hold you have over me.
For the company you keep,
Is a reflection, truly.

I'll forever and ever, remember,
Our rather late nigh time convos
And fits of giggles.

Our bouts of screams,
And wounding clashes

Yet, we have the same dream,
Unity.

Family

I do realise I'm lucky,
Luckier than most.

I do realise it can be rocky,
Akin to most.

I understand we have many differences,
But don't we all?

I understand we have principles,
And we each play a role.
We're a unit after all.

Some families are uniform.
Mum, dad and kids.
But others don't really conform,

Boundaries can be muddled, but joined with
love.
As long as we understand each other, that's a
must.

Patience, also comes a long way.
But remember, don't eat my food I've stashed
away!!

IDKY

I watched a TED talk recently
On how the mind of a master procrastinator
works
And apparently, there's a panic monster inside of
me?

I'm forever trapped in this 'dark playground'
It's as though I have nowhere else to turn!
With my panic monster, lurking in the shadows,
ready to jump!

I'm not sure why I need adrenaline to push me to
complete tasks.
Why can't I be normal and complete it on time
instead?

This stress is really no good for me!

Trust the Process

Patience is a virtue,
which unfortunately,
many don't possess.

The hard truth here is,
That no matter how much effort you put in
You have to wait sometimes.

And that, my friends,
Is an important lesson.

God knows when things are right for you.
When it's the right time.

So just wait,
Hang on
and trust the process.

www.ingramcontent.com/pod-product-compliance
Lightning Source LLC
LaVergne TN
LVHW051241200726
843510LV00011B/1644